Connect the correct carriage with the matching clown at the top.
Look carefully at the colors!

Find the five differences between the pictures and circle them.

Can you find the puzzle pieces shown at the bottom in the picture above?
Circle the matching pieces of the puzzle.

Color the picture to match the color of the dots.

Can you trace the waves with your pencil?

Draw the objects shown at the bottom of the page where they belong in the picture.

Can you find in the pictures the objects shown at the bottom of the page? Connect the objects to the picture with a line.

Every object appears twice on this page. Link the pairs with a line.

Draw the objects that the clown would put in his bag.

Look for three matching flowers in a row and draw a line through them.

Decorate the cake with icing, candles and cherries.

Repair the cages by finishing the bars with your pencil.

Draw and color the last bird in the row.

Circle the flower that doesn't match in the row.

How can the rabbit reach the carrots? Draw a line along the path that follows the clues at the top of the page.

How can the tortoise reach the lettuce? Draw the path.

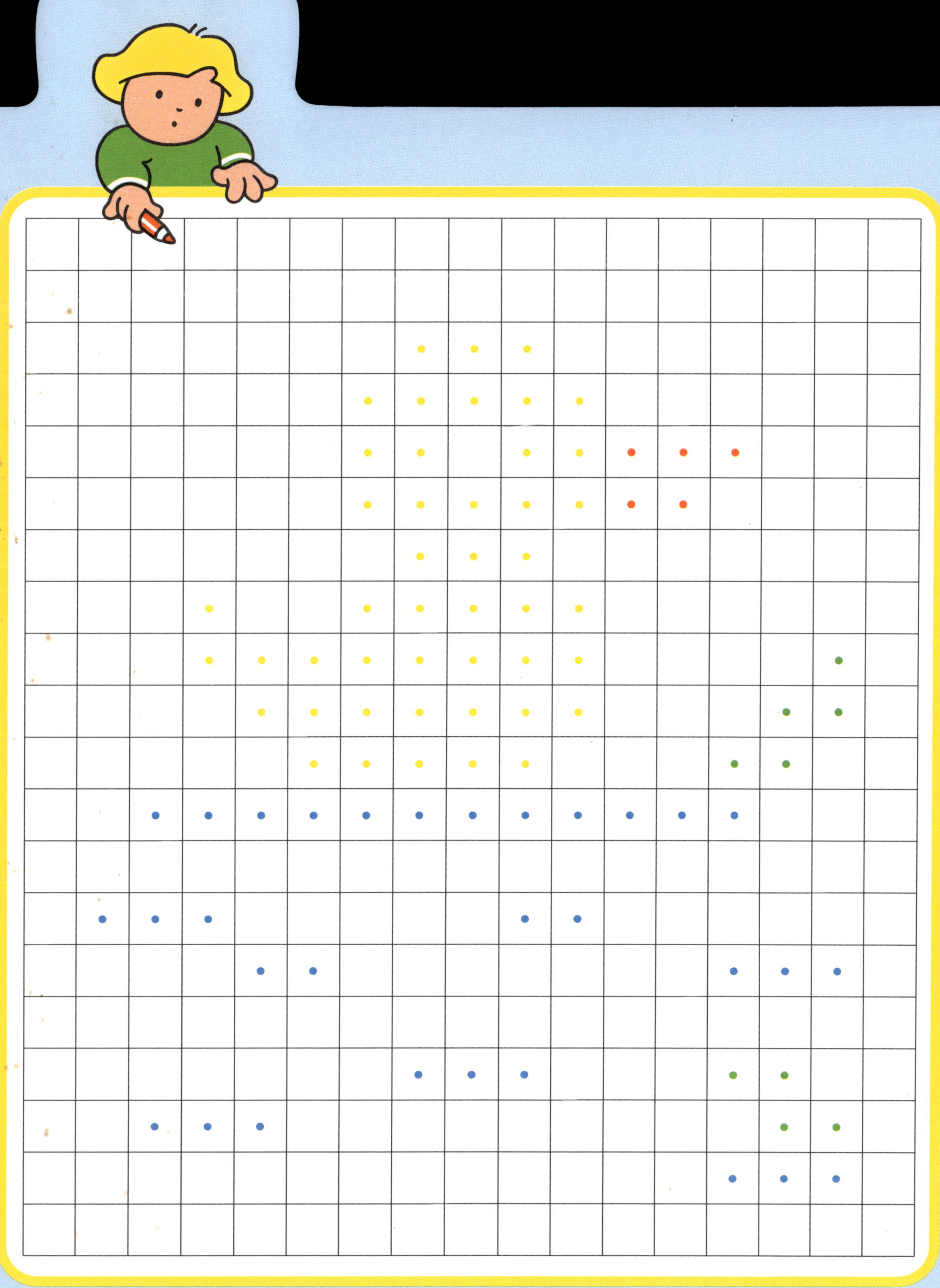

Color the squares the same color of the spots to find out what the hidden picture is!

Which socks match? Connect the pairs with a line.

Draw a pretty bunch of flowers in the vase.

Color the clothes with a zipper red. Color the clothes with buttons blue.

Find the five differences. When you have finished, color in the bottom picture to match the top.

Beginning at the top, color in the paths to the bottom. Which rabbit finds the most carrots on its way?

Draw colored pebbles or buttons on the snowman.

Both clowns wear the same clothes. Color the clown to match his friend.

What does Tiny the Mouse catch in his net? Draw it above the flowers.

Six birds are hidden in the picture. Can you find them?

Color the picture to match the color of the dots.

The rabbit goes home skipping. Draw the path that leads her by the most apple trees.

Color in the three pictures so that they look the same.

How can the dog reach the shepherd? Draw the path.

Find the five differences. When you have finished, color in the bottom picture.

Draw a fisherman in the boat.